Listen to

A book of 30 Bible readings and notes
to help you worship and pray

Tony Phelps-Jones

Published by Scripture Union, 207–209 Queensway, Bletchley, MK2 2EB, England.
Email: info@scriptureunion.org.uk
Internet: www.scriptureunion.org.uk

© Copyright all editions Causeway Prospects
First published in 2008
ISBN 978 1 84427 306 5

Causeway Prospects is a division of Prospects for People with Learning Disabilities and their address is 69 Honey End Lane, Reading, RG30 4EL. Phone 0118 9516 978. Email: causeway@prospects.org.uk Website: www.prospects.org.uk

About Causeway Prospects: Causeway Prospects provides resource materials and training to equip churches for effective outreach and ministry among people with learning disabilities. It also runs holiday weekends and special ministry at Spring Harvest and the Keswick Convention.

British Library Cataloguing-in-Publication Data: a catalogue record for this book is available from the British Library.

Scripture portions are taken from The Holy Bible: English Version for the Deaf (published as the Easy-to-Read Version) © 2000 by the World Bible Translation Center, Inc. and used with permission. Internet: www.wbtc.com

Icons © Widgit Software Ltd 2002, developed by the Rebus Symbol Development Project, designed by Cate Detheridge and used with kind permission.

Cover design by David Lund Design: www.davidlund-design.com

Internal page layout by Creative Pages: www.creativepages.org.uk

Printed and bound in Singapore by Tien Wah Press

Scripture Union is an international charity working with churches in more than 130 countries providing resources to bring the good news about Jesus Christ to children, young people and families – and to encourage them to develop spiritually through the Bible and prayer. As well as a network of volunteers, staff and associates who run holidays, church-based events and school Christian groups, we produce a wide range of publications and support those who use our resources through training programmes.

Using this book

 Listen to Jesus! and the other titles in this series are intended to help you to worship and pray. On each page there is a reading from the Bible, some thoughts and a prayer.

 The readings are from the *Easy-to-Read Version* (ETRV), a very clear and simple translation of the Bible. The reading printed each day is quite short. A longer reading is also given if you would like to read more using your own Bible. There is a list of key words and their meanings near the back of the book.

Reading the Bible

The Bible, which is sometimes called the Word of God, is not really one book but a whole library of many books. The 66 books were written by many people who God spoke to at different times. At the front of the Bible you will find a list of the titles of all the books in the Bible and the page number where each book begins.

To help you find your way around such a big book, little groups of one or two sentences have been numbered, and then groups of those sentences have been collected into chapters.

So how do you find the one or two sentences that you want in the Bible? Let's say you want to find Matthew 5:5,6. That means you need to look in the book called Matthew, in chapter number 5 and verses 5 and 6.

You can find Matthew in the list of books at the front of the Bible. This tells you which page Matthew starts on. When you have turned to the beginning of Matthew you then search for chapter 5. Look down the page until you see the numbers 5 and 6. Those are the sentences (or verses) that you need.

When you do your Bible reading, try to spend a few extra minutes praying and worshipping. Praying is talking and listening to God. You can do this aloud or without using words. You can pray on your own or with friends. Worship is telling God how much you love him, through words or songs, or things you do. This can be singing in church, but it's a lot more than that. It's about enjoying the wonderful world God has made. It's about how we speak to each other. It's about how we live our lives.

As you pray you can:

 thank God for his goodness and his help;

 tell God how great he is, and that you love him;

 ask God to help you, your friends, your family and other people.

If you are a helper using this book with someone who does not read, you will find guidance notes at the end.

The *Easy-to-Read Version* of the Bible is available to buy from Causeway Prospects.

Listen to Jesus!

1 Listening

Jesus taught the people. He said, 'What great blessings there are for the people that [know they] have spiritual needs! The kingdom of heaven belongs to them.'
Matthew 5:2,3 (Full reading Matthew 5:1–3)

Crowds of people came to listen to Jesus. They sat on the hillside while Jesus spoke. What Jesus said was wonderful.

This booklet is about listening to Jesus. We cannot listen to Jesus like those people did in today's Bible verses. But the Bible tells us what Jesus said. So when we read the Bible, or hear it read, it is like listening to Jesus. What Jesus said is still wonderful.

Dear God, thank you that what Jesus said is written down for us in the Bible. Please help me to learn a lot as I read this book. Amen.

2   Follow me!

Jesus said, 'Come follow me. I will make you [a different kind of] fishermen. You will work to gather people, not fish.'
Matthew 4:19 (Full reading Matthew 4:18–20)

One of the first things Jesus did was to invite some fishermen to go with him. 'Follow me', said Jesus. The men became Jesus' followers or disciples. They went everywhere with Jesus. They watched what Jesus did and learned from him. Then they started doing the same things as Jesus.

Jesus wants us all to be followers too. We need to find out from the Bible what Jesus said. Then we can start to do the same things that Jesus did.

Dear Lord Jesus, I want to follow you. Help me to be a really good follower. Amen.

3 Son of God

 Then Jesus said to his followers, 'And who do you say I am?' Simon Peter answered, 'You are the Christ, the Son of the living God.' Matthew 16:15,16 (Full reading Matthew 16:15–17)

 The people in the crowds were not sure who Jesus was. So Jesus asked his followers. Peter spoke up. Peter said, 'You are the Son of the living God.' Jesus said, 'Well done, Peter! That's the right answer.'

Peter and the other followers were sure about who Jesus was. What about you? If you are not sure about Jesus being the Son of God, pray about that today.

 Dear God, please send your Holy Spirit to help me to be sure about who Jesus is. Amen.

4   I am the way

**Jesus answered, 'I am the way. I am the truth
and the life. The only way to the Father is
through me.'**
John 14:6 (Full reading John 14:5,6)

Jesus was talking to his followers about God's family.
In God's family, God is the Father of Jesus. God can
be our Father too. For God to be our Father, we
must believe that Jesus is the Son of God. Then we
can ask God to make us his child – his son or his
daughter.

If you, or your friend, want to join God's family, you
can say today's prayer.

**Dear Father God, thank you that Jesus is your
Son. Please send your Holy Spirit to make me
into your son (or your daughter). And stay
with me forever. Amen.**

5   Turn from sin

The woman answered, 'None of them judged me, sir.' Then Jesus said, 'So I also don't judge you. You can go now, but don't sin again.'
John 8:11   (Full reading John 8:4,7,10,11)

This story began with a woman doing something bad. The people who caught her wanted to kill her. Jesus stopped the people from killing her. Then Jesus told the woman not to do bad things any more.

The Bible calls bad things like this 'sins'. When we do sins it makes God sad. God does not want us to do those things. Whenever Jesus talked to people he said, 'Turn away from doing bad things. Stop it now!'

Dear God, please show me anything I do that is wrong and makes you sad. Help me to stop doing it. Amen.

6   Love the Lord

Jesus answered, 'You must love the Lord your God. You must love him with all your heart, all your soul, and all your mind.'
Matthew 22:37 (Full reading Matthew 22:35–37)

Jesus was asked which was the most important commandment. 'Love God' was Jesus' answer. And he said we must love God with all our heart, all our soul and all our mind. In other words, we must love God with all of us, with every bit of us.

We can show that we love God by worshipping him. We can show our love by trusting God, and by praying to him. As we go on through this book, we'll be finding out more ways to show our love for God.

Dear God, I do love you. Help me to do things every day that show how much I love you. Amen.

7 Do what I say

'If you love me, then you will do the things I command. I will ask the Father, and he will give you another Helper. He will give you this Helper to be with you forever.'
John 14:15,16 (Full reading John 14:15–17)

Jesus said, 'If you love me, you will do what I say.' It is a sign of our love for a person that we are willing to do things to help them. Sometimes it is not easy to do that. That is why Jesus talks about a Helper. The Holy Spirit is that Helper, helping us to do what Jesus says.

Is there something you are finding difficult? Use today's prayer to ask for help.

Dear God, I want to do what Jesus says. Please send your Holy Spirit to help me. Amen.

8 Loving others

And the second command is like the first: 'You must love other people the same as you love yourself.'
Matthew 22:39 (Full reading Matthew 22:37–39)

Jesus told a story to explain who our neighbour is: the story of the good Samaritan. In the story, a man was attacked. Two people walked past and didn't help. The third person did help. That third person was the good Samaritan.

Jesus said that anyone who needs help is our neighbour. We should be looking out for people we can show love to by helping them. What a difference you could make by offering help to someone who is having a bit of trouble!

Dear God, help me to notice when people are having trouble. Show me how I can help. Amen.

9 Serving others

'The Son of Man did not come for other people to serve him. The Son of Man came to serve other people. The Son of Man came to give his life to save many people.'
Matthew 20:28 (Full reading Matthew 20:26–28)

Jesus is the Son of God. Jesus worked with God to make the world and everything in it. Jesus is more powerful than any person on earth. But Jesus says he came to serve. And he wants us to be servants too.

What is a servant like? A servant clears the tea things away before sitting down to watch TV. A servant makes sure everyone is comfy in their seats on the minibus before finding their own seat.

Lord God, please send your Holy Spirit to teach me how to be a servant, so I can serve other people well. Amen.

10 Doing good

'Live so that people will see the good things you do. Live so that people will praise your Father in heaven.'
Matthew 5:16 (Full reading Matthew 5:15,16)

Praise means talking or singing about how great God is. It's an important part of our lives as followers of Jesus. But we want other people to praise God too.

When we do good things, when we serve other people, it can help them to think about God. If we are filled with the joy of the Lord as we serve others, it will show. Then our friends may join with us in giving thanks and praise to God.

Dear God, help me to show your joy and share your joy with others as I serve them. Amen.

11 Don't worry

Look at the birds. They don't plant or harvest or save food in barns. But your heavenly Father feeds those birds. And you know that you are worth much more than the birds. You cannot add any time to your life by worrying about it.
Matthew 6:26,27 (Full reading Matthew 6:25–27)

Jesus knows that some people worry a lot. But Jesus says there is no need to worry. People are worth much more than birds, but God makes sure that all the birds have enough to eat.

Some people worry about clothes or food, some worry about money or music CDs or cars. They spend ages thinking and talking about these things. Jesus says there are more important things to think about.

Dear God, help me to trust you and not worry. Amen.

12 Don't be afraid

... the followers saw Jesus walking on the water. They thought he was a ghost. The followers shouted with fear ... But Jesus spoke to the followers and said, 'Don't worry! It's me! Don't be afraid.'
Mark 6:49,50 (Full reading Mark 6:47–51)

This must have been very frightening for Jesus' followers. It was the middle of the night. They were trying to row their boat against a strong wind. They were exhausted. Then they saw what looked like a ghost walking towards them.

Things can happen to frighten us. It might be a thunderstorm or an angry dog. Being alone can be scary if we hear a noise outside. We can be frightened by other people, or by spiders.

Dear God, whenever I am frightened, help me to know that you are with me. Amen.

13 Jesus dying

 Jesus said to the followers, 'The Son of Man will be given into the control of men. Those men will kill the Son of Man.'
Matthew 17:22,23 (Full reading Matthew 17:22,23)

 Jesus knew what was going to happen. Jesus told his followers that he was going to be killed. Jesus knew who would kill him and how.

When the Roman soldiers killed Jesus, it was horrible. It was a sad day. But we must remember this: it was part of God's plan. Jesus was doing what God wanted him to do. It was the only way that our sins – the bad things we do – could be forgiven. Jesus gave his life for us.

 Dear God, thank you that Jesus did what you wanted him to do. Help me to do what you want me to do. Amen.

14 It is finished

Later, Jesus knew that everything had been done ... Then he said, 'It is finished.' Jesus bowed his head and died.
John 19:28,30 (Full reading John 19:28–30)

Jesus had spent his life on earth telling people about God. Jesus had been showing God's love to people. Now Jesus was dying on the cross.

Jesus knew he had done everything his Father God wanted. By dying like this, he showed God's love for every single person in the world. Jesus' job was done. He could say, 'It is finished.'

Let's use the words of this song as our prayer today:
> **Jesus has died for me and for you;**
> **Given us life and breath, made us new;**
> **Taken away our sin and shame;**
> **Wonderful Saviour, we worship you.**

15 Forgive them

Jesus said, 'Father, forgive these people [that are killing me]. They don't know what they are doing.'
Luke 23:34 (Full reading Luke 23:32–34)

Jesus looked down from the cross. He saw the soldiers who nailed him to the cross. He saw the Jewish leaders who were against him. All those people needed God's forgiveness. Jesus said 'Father, forgive them.'

We all need God's forgiveness. When we say sorry to God for doing wrong things, God forgives us. God will not remember those things any more, or be cross about them. God will not punish us – Jesus has taken the punishment instead of us.

Dear God, I am sorry for the things I have said or done that have hurt other people and upset you. Please forgive me. Amen.

16 Remember me

... Jesus said, 'This bread is my body that I am giving for you. Eat this to remember me.'
Luke 22:19 (Full reading Luke 22:19,20)

The night before Jesus died he had a special meal with his friends. It was a meal for a special time of year called Passover. This meal is sometimes called 'the Last Supper'. Jesus took some bread and gave it to his followers. Jesus said, 'Eat this to remember me.' Then he gave them some wine to drink.

Most churches have services with bread and wine. This service might be called Holy Communion, the Lord's Supper, Eucharist or Breaking of Bread. When we eat the bread and drink the wine or juice we remember that Jesus died for us.

Dear God, thank you that Jesus' body was broken and Jesus' blood poured out for me. Amen.

17 In trouble

'In this world you will have trouble. But be brave! I have defeated the world!'
John 16:33 (Full reading John 16:33)

Some people think that when you believe in Jesus, you will always be happy. Nothing will ever go wrong. But Jesus did not say that. Sometimes bad things do happen to Christians. People get sick. People lose their jobs. People get hurt in accidents.

What Jesus did say is, 'I will be with you.' That's one of the great things about being a Christian. Even when life is hard, God is with us. God helps us to make the best of difficult times.

Dear God, please give your strength to me (or my friend) when I am having difficult days. Amen.

18 Help is here

'I will ask the Father, and he will give you another Helper. He will give you this Helper to be with you forever ... I told you these things so that you can have peace in me.'
John 14:16; 16:33 (Full reading John 14:16; 16:33)

One of the things God's Holy Spirit does is to give us peace. That does not mean that everything will be quiet. It does not mean we will always sleep well! Having God's peace means that when things are difficult, we are not worried or frightened.

This is something we can tell other people about. God does not like people feeling bad. If you have a friend who is worried, frightened or upset, tell them that God's Holy Spirit can give them peace.

Father God, please send your Holy Spirit to give my friend (say their name) peace and make them feel better. Amen.

19 'I am there ... '

**'... if two or three people are together
believing in me, I am there with them.'**
Matthew 18:20 (Full reading Matthew 18:19,20)

Praying is always a good thing to do. You can pray
on your own. You can pray with other people.
Jesus says whenever you meet with somebody to
pray, he is there with you.

When you pray with others you can first talk about
what you want to pray about. Then you can agree
on what to pray for and agree about how to pray.

God will always hear our prayers. We can trust
him to answer our prayers in the way that is best
for the people we are praying for.

**Pray right now for members of your family
or close friends.**

20 Ask, seek, knock

'Continue to ask, and God will give to you. Continue to search, and you will find. Continue to knock, and the door will open for you.'
Matthew 7:7 (Full reading Matthew 7:7,8)

'Continue to ask' means 'go on asking'. If you want to know something, keep asking questions until you get the answer. When you are praying, don't give up! Sometimes people pray for others for many, many years before they believe in Jesus.

Do you know this song about prayer?

> Ask, ask, ask and he will give it to you.
> Seek, seek, seek and you will find.
> Knock, knock, knock and the door will be opened.
> For Father loves to give to you.

Dear God, please send your Holy Spirit to help me to keep on praying. Amen.

21 Jesus gives rest

'Come to me all you people that are tired and have heavy burdens. I will give you rest.'
Matthew 11:28 (Full reading Matthew 11:28,29)

Lots of people these days are in a rush. They dash from one job to the next. There's always too much to do and not enough time to do it. When you ask, they might say, 'I'm worn out!' Jesus says, 'Come to me all you people that are tired.'

Jesus wants us to come to him to listen and to learn. Jesus wants us to stop rushing for a while and give him some of our time. Then, says Jesus, 'I will give you rest.'

Dear Lord Jesus, help me to find time to be with you so that you can give me rest. Amen.

22 Kingdom come

'We pray that your kingdom will come, and that the things you want will be done here on earth, the same as in heaven.'
Matthew 6:10 (Full reading Matthew 6:9,10)

This is part of the prayer that Jesus taught to his followers. We call it 'The Lord's Prayer'. In heaven things happen exactly as God wants them to. This prayer asks that things here on earth should happen as God wants them to.

This is a good prayer to pray. And we can be part of the answer to this prayer. As we find out what God wants, and do those things, God's kingdom will come more and more.

Dear God, please help me to do things that will make your kingdom come on earth. Amen.

23 Temptation

'Don't let us be tempted (tested); but save us from the Evil One (the devil).'
Matthew 6:13 (Full reading Matthew 6:11–13)

Being tempted is when you feel like doing something wrong. If somebody makes you cross, you might feel like hitting them. That's temptation. It would be wrong to hit them. So you don't do it.

If you see a £20 note on the floor in a shop, do you pick it up and keep it? No! You hand it in.

The Evil One (the devil) is God's enemy and our enemy. He will try to make us do all kinds of wrong things. Keep praying this part of the Lord's Prayer, and say 'no' to temptation.

Dear God, please help me to do the right thing all the time. Amen.

24 Treasure

'Don't save treasures for yourselves here on earth. Moths and rust will destroy treasures here on earth ... The treasures in heaven cannot be destroyed ... '
Matthew 6:19,20 (Full reading Matthew 6:19,20)

In stories like Pirates of the Caribbean, the pirates look for treasure – lots of money and things made of gold. Some people spend all their lives making lots of money. They buy houses, cars and other things that cost lots of money. That's their treasure.

The treasures in heaven that Jesus talks about come from things we do that please God. Helping other people, praying for friends, forgiving people when they hurt us... Doing things like these makes treasure that will last for ever.

Dear God, help me to do things that make treasure in heaven. Amen.

25 A place for you

'There are many rooms in my Father's house. I would not tell you this if it were not true. I am going there to prepare a place for you.'
John 14:2 (Full reading John 14:1–3)

Jesus was talking about heaven. He was soon going back to heaven to get a place ready for all his followers. Every person who believes in Jesus and loves the Father God will have their own special place in heaven.

Heaven is a wonderful place. If you are a follower of Jesus, you will go there one day. Heaven will be full of God's people. They will welcome you with cheers and shouts of joy.

Dear Father God, thank you for the promise of heaven. Help me to be ready to go there one day. Amen.

26 In heaven

'Come up here, and I will show you what must happen after this.' ... There before me was a throne in heaven.
Revelation 4:1,2 (Full reading Revelation 4:1–3)

Jesus told a man called John to come and see what heaven was like. Heaven is an amazing place. Jesus is there, and everything and every person in heaven is worshipping Jesus. It is the most beautiful place that anyone has ever seen.

In heaven there will be no crying or sadness, no pain or hurting. Everybody will be able to understand what you say. Nobody will be rude. There will be joy on every face.

Dear God, please help me to talk to someone today about how wonderful heaven is. Amen.

27 Forever with Jesus

Yes, God loved the world so much that he gave his only Son. God gave his Son so that every person that believes in him would not be lost, but have life forever.
John 3:16 (Full reading John 3:16,17)

This is the best known verse in the whole Bible. God offers the gift of life to everybody. Lots of people do not know what to do with their lives. They do not know the most important thing about life. The most important thing in life is to believe in Jesus and to follow him. People who do that will enjoy life with God. It will be a great life on earth first, then in heaven forever.

Dear God, please help me to talk about you and Jesus with my friends. Amen.

28 Coming again

'Then people will see the Son of Man coming in the clouds with power and great glory.'
Mark 13:26 (Full reading Mark 13:26,27)

Jesus came to the earth as a baby and grew up to be a man. When Jesus had finished doing everything God wanted him to do, Jesus went back to heaven. One day Jesus will come back to the earth. People call that 'the second coming'. Nobody knows when that will happen.

When Jesus comes back he will talk to us. He will ask us about our lives. You will be able to tell Jesus about your love for him. You will be able to tell Jesus how you showed his love to other people.

Dear God, please help me to be ready when Jesus comes back. Amen.

Before these things happen, the good news must be told to all people.
Mark 13:10 (Full reading Mark 13:10,11)

Something has to happen before Jesus can come back. It's this: the good news about Jesus must be told to people all over the world. People in every country on earth need to know that Jesus loves them.

Some people spend their lives going to other countries to tell people about Jesus. We call those people missionaries. Sometimes things are difficult or dangerous for them. People who do missionary work need God's help and our prayers every day.

In your prayers today think of anybody you know who is working in another country telling people about Jesus.

30 Tell others

... God gave us the work of bringing people into peace with him.
2 Corinthians 5:18 (Full reading 2 Corinthians 5:18)

Every follower of Jesus has a job to do. That job is to help other people to get to know God. That's what Jesus did. Jesus told people about God. Jesus showed people the love of God.

So that's our job. To tell people about Jesus. And to show people the love of God. Jesus will send his Holy Spirit to help us. And the angels in heaven shout for joy whenever a new person starts to believe in Jesus.

Dear God, please help other people to believe in Jesus when I talk to them. Thank you, Lord. Amen.

Key words

Amen   We usually say this at the end of prayers and it means, 'That's my prayer too'.

Blessings   Good things from God.

Commandment   Something you have to do or obey. It's like a rule or order.

Defeated   Beaten in a fight or competition or game.

Follow/follower   People who find out what Jesus wants them to do, then they do those things.

Forgive/Forgiveness   When you forgive someone who has hurt you you're not cross with them anymore.

Gather   Collect together.

Heaven   Where God the Father and Jesus live.

Helper   Someone who helps another. The Holy Spirit sometimes has this name.

Holy Spirit   The Holy Spirit is a person. The Holy Spirit is God at work on the earth.

Joy   A happy feeling that fills your heart and makes you want to smile or laugh.

Judge   A judge is a person who decides if someone has done wrong.

Kingdom   A place or country where a king is in charge.

Lord   The one in charge. Another word for God.

Passover   A Jewish holiday when people remember how the angel of death passed by Jewish houses without hurting people.

Peace/peaceful   Quiet, calm, not worrying.

Praise   Telling God how great and good he is.

Pray   To talk to God or Jesus about things.

Punish/punishment   What happens to a person caught doing wrong things.

Servant   Someone who does everything that another person wants them to.

Shame   The bad feeling people get after doing wrong things.

Sin/sins   Things people do that make God sad and hurt other people.

Soul   Like a person's spirit, deep inside. It's the part of a person that God can touch and change.

Spiritual   To do with the part inside people that helps them listen to God and do what he wants. It's about being a friend of God.

Treasure   Something precious, valuable and important.

Worship   Telling God how much you love him through words or songs or things you do.

38

Notes for carers and helpers

These Bible guides are designed to help a wide range of people who need extra help. It's impossible to tailor Bible notes to fit everyone's needs. But our hope is that many who have some level of visual or intellectual disability or just need a simpler approach can be helped to pray and read the Bible regularly through this series.

Some people will be able to use these notes without any help from others. But if you are the carer or helper of someone needing some assistance with using them, here are a few pointers which may be useful to you.

Before you begin, ask the Holy Spirit to help communicate the main thought from each reading and note to the person you are reading with. God through the Holy Spirit can communicate on levels that we cannot! Part of the Holy Spirit's role is to make Jesus real to people and you are working in partnership with him.

Make sure you have the person's full attention before starting to read. Think about how you can eliminate auditory or visual distractions in the environment such as TV or other people's conversations. Try to find a quiet place. Use eye contact to maintain good connection.

Read slowly and clearly, pausing where suitable. Facial expressions, hand and body movements can all help to underline the meaning of the material. Encourage whatever response is appropriate, particularly in prayer and praise.

Use your knowledge of the person to assess how much is being understood, how much clarification might be needed and how best to make applications more relevant.

Make your time together an opportunity for learning and fellowship for both of you.

Other titles in the Bible Prospects series:

Being like Jesus

Come, Holy Spirit!

David pleased God

God gives new life

In the beginning

Moses, man of God

Paul followed God

Songs of praise

The first Christians

The story of Christmas

The story of Easter

Bible Prospects on audio All these titles are available as audio CDs by mail order direct from Causeway Prospects (address on page 2).

Scripture Union produces a wide range of Bible reading notes for people of all ages and Bible-based material for small groups. SU publications are available from Christian bookshops. For information and to request free samples and a free catalogue of Bible resources:

✧   phone SU's mail order line: local rate number 08450 706006

✧   email info@scriptureunion.org.uk

✧   log on to www.scriptureunion.org.uk

✧   write to SU Mail Order, PO Box 5148, Milton Keynes MLO, MK2 2YX